DESTINATION
GERMAN

Illustrated Phrasebook
& Travel Information

**Kate Corney and
Mike Buckby**

NTC Publishing Group
Lincolnwood, Illinois USA

Book and Tapescript by
Kate Corney and Mike Buckby
Cassettes produced by Footstep Productions Ltd

Destination German was produced in collaboration with
the Language Teaching Centre at the
University of York

Picture credits
Austrian Federal Railways page 83;
Austrian National Tourist Office page 86;
Robert Harding Picture Library page 90;
Image Bank (Hans Wolf) page 74;
Zefa Picture Library pages 69 and 70.

This edition first published in 1996 by
NTC Publishing Group,
4255 W. Touhy Avenue, Lincolnwood, Illinois, USA 60646-1975.
© Teresa Huntley and Mike Buckby 1993
Published in co-operation with BBC Worldwide Limited.
"BBC" and the BBC logotype are trademarks of the
British Broadcasting Corporation, and are used under licence.

Printed in Hong Kong.

5 6 7 8 9 0 WKT 9 8 7 6 5 4 3 2 1

CONTENTS
THE GERMAN LANGUAGE

GERMANY AND AUSTRIA

HOW TO USE THIS BOOK

WELCOME TO *DESTINATION GERMAN!*

This book has been designed to help young
people like you. It will help you when you go to
Germany (**Deutschland**) or Austria (**Österreich**).
It will also help you if you learn German at
school and want some extra practice.

The book is pocket-sized so you can carry it
around with you while you are on vacation. It
contains the language and information that
you'll need to help you to enjoy your stay abroad.

When you are talking with German-speaking
people you will only be easily understood if you
pronounce things properly. To help you do this
better, there are also two cassettes designed for
use with the book. But don't worry if you don't
have them, because the book and cassettes can
also be used separately. The cassettes allow you
to repeat phrases and to listen to German-
speaking people to see if you can understand
them.

The *Destination German* Book

The book is divided into two sections. The first is
about the language, and the second is about
Germany and Austria.
The language section contains:
1. Some *key phrases* to get you started.
2. Twelve useful "situations" (**Themen**).
3. A list of additional *useful words and phrases.*

You can start with **Thema eins** and work through to **Thema zwölf**. Or, if you prefer, you can work on the situations in any order, as you need them. In each **Thema** you will find:

1. *Key Phrases*

   These are the main phrases you'll need to help you in the situation. Try to learn them before you move on to the next section. One way of doing this is to copy them several times. When you feel confident, cover up the German. Look at the English phrase, write the German for it from memory, then check to see if you were right. Don't worry if you don't get them all right the first time. Take a break, then try to learn those which gave you trouble. Your cassettes will also help you learn the phrases. Practice saying each one after the recording until you feel confident.

2. *Conversations*

   These are made up of the key phrases. Read them to see if you understand them.

3. *Find Out More*

   This will give you more information about the language and give you the power to say more.

4. *Over To You*

   This is your big chance to see how much you know. Try the exercises. All the answers are at the end of the unit. DON'T CHEAT! Only look at the answers AFTER you have done the exercise.

   If you work through the **Thema** in this way, you should feel quite confident.

Visiting Germany and Austria

The second section of the book tells you more about Germany and Austria. It contains:

1. *Maps* of Germany and Austria
2. *Information* on towns
3. *Practical tips* linked to the twelve Themen
4. *Quizzes* to see how much you've learned

The *Destination German* Cassettes

This is very important for your learning.
Sometimes you will find exercises in your book that refer to the cassettes. You need to practice saying the phrases just as much as you need to practice writing them.
SO . . . USE THE CASSETTES WELL!
The cassettes contain the twelve **Themen** and link directly with them.
For each **Thema** on the cassettes there are:

1. *Listen and Repeat*
   These are the key phrases which you will find on the first page of each unit.
   - Listen to the recording of each phrase.
   - Find the phrase on the first page of the unit.
   - Point to it as you hear it.
   - Rewind your cassette (remember to make a note of the counter number to save you time when you want to rewind).
   - Listen again and repeat each phrase. Do this at least three or four times, or as often as you wish, until you become confident.

- Cover up the German in your book.
- Repeat the phrase once more.
- Finally try to say the phrase at the same time as the tape, without looking at the book.

2. *Spot the Word/Listen, Understand and Repeat*
   This section gives you the opportunity to practice saying the phrases again, but they will be in a different order from the book. With very long words, you are given special tasks to help you learn to say them really well.

3. *Conversations*
   These are the conversations on the second page of each unit. Listen to them and follow them in your book. You can then practice saying them:
   - first after the cassette.
   - then at the same time as the cassette.
   Finally, read the conversations aloud without the help of the cassette.

4. *Listen and Understand*
   You can now practice understanding German-speaking people using the phrases you have just learned.

5. *Over to You*
   This last section gives you the chance to show what you know. You can practice using the phrases you have learned in conversations. Often there will be a gap in the recording. You should speak in this gap. At first you'll probably want to pause the cassette to do this. Practice until you become quick enough to fill the gap without pausing the cassette. The answer is recorded immediately after the gap.

TO GET YOU STARTED

Willkommen! Before you start to learn your situations, here are some basic words which you could use in many conversations. These words are recorded on the cassettes. Learn them and they will help you when you talk with people in Germany and Austria.

Practice repeating the words after you have heard them on the cassette. It's a good idea to try to learn them in groups of three.

Guten Morgen.	Good Morning.
Guten Tag.	Hello, Good Day.
Guten Abend.	Good Evening.
Grüß Gott.	Hello (You'll find that people use this in South Germany and Austria).
Auf Wiedersehen.	Goodbye.
Bis später.	See you later.
Ja.	Yes.
Nein.	No.
Danke.	Thank you.
Bitte.	Please.
Bitte?	Pardon?
Ich verstehe nicht.	I don't understand.
Ich weiß nicht.	I don't know.
Wie heißt das auf englisch?	What's that in English?
Wie heißt das auf deutsch?	What's that in German?
Können Sie bitte langsamer sprechen?	Can you speak more slowly?
Können Sie das bitte wiederholen?	Can you repeat that, please?

Wie schreibt man das?   How do you write that?

und	and
auch	also
dort drüben	over there
aber	but
ich heiße...	I'm called...

Here's an idea to help you learn these phrases:
Copy them once. Look at the first six. Read
them through six times. Now cover up the
German. How many can you write out in
German? Check your answers. Now use the
same method to learn again any you had
problems with. Finally, do the same with the
other phrases here. Use this method to learn
the phrases in each unit.

ASKING THE WAY

One of the first things you might need to do when you arrive in Germany or Austria is to ask the way. You will need to stop a passer-by and ask for help.

TIP	Remember – SMILE. BE POLITE. SPEAK CLEARLY.

DON'T BE AFRAID TO ASK THEM TO REPEAT WHAT THEY SAY AND SHOW YOUR THANKS BY SAYING **DANKE SCHÖN**.

KEY PHRASES

Entschuldigen Sie, bitte.	Excuse me, please.
Wo ist die Post?	Where's the post office?
Wo ist der Bahnhof?	Where's the station?
Wo ist das Verkehrsamt?	Where's the information office?
Wo ist das Einkaufszentrum?	Where's the shopping center?
Sie gehen geradeaus.	You go straight ahead (on).
Sie gehen links.	You go left.
Sie gehen geradeaus und dann rechts.	You go straight ahead (on) a then right.
Sie nehmen die erste Straße rechts.	Take the first street on the right.
Sie nehmen die zweite Straße links.	Take the second street on the left.
Ist es weit?	Is it far?
Es ist fünf Minuten von hier.	It is five minutes from here.

Richard and Emma are staying in a German town.

Richard asks for directions.

Find Out More

1. In German there are three words for "the:"
der, die and **das**. When you learn a new word in German, it's a good idea to learn the right word for "the" at the same time. So, rather than just learning that the German for station is
"Bahnhof," learn <u>der</u> Bahnhof. Similarly: <u>die</u> Post, <u>das</u> Verkehrsamt, <u>das</u> Einkaufszentrum.

2. Here are some directions you could be given:

Gegenüber dem Bahnhof.	Opposite the station.
Vor der Post.	In front of the post office.
Neben dem Café.	Next to the café.
Gehen Sie bis zur Ampel.	Go to the traffic lights.

Listen to your cassette to practice these.

Over To You

1. You may see these symbols in town. Write down the names of the places they are directing you to.

2. You are spending a few days in Freiburg, a town in the Black Forest in South Germany.
(a) On the first day you decide to go to the information office to get a town map. How would you ask the way there?
(b) At the information office you decide you would like to go shopping. How would you ask to find the way to the shopping center?

(c) You buy a postcard and want to mail it. How would you ask the way to the post office?
(d) Finally, you need to get some train times for a trip the next day. How would you ask the way to the station?

Write your answers to question 2 once. Check them below and then say them ten times.

3. You are giving directions. Write what you would say for each of these.

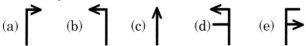

(a)　　(b)　　(c)　　(d)　　(e)

4. You see these signs in the side mirror of your bus. Write down what they are.

(a) **BAHNHOF** (b) **EINKAUFSZENTRUM**

(c) **VERKEHRSAMT** (d) **POST**

Now write down how you would ask the way to these places.

Check your answers below. Then cover them up and say them all from memory, using only the mirror words to help you.

SHOPPING FOR FOOD

When you are in Germany or Austria you'll want to buy some of the local foods. If you go on day trips you'll probably take a picnic. The easiest place to buy your food is the local supermarket, but you'll still need to ask for some items. Many towns have a market where you can find a good selection of fruit and salads.

KEY PHRASES

Bitte sehr?	Can I help you?
Ich möchte...	I would like...
Zwei Brötchen.	Two bread rolls.
Hundert Gramm Käse.	One hundred grams of cheese.
Sechs Scheiben Salami.	Six slices of salami.
Ein Pfund Tomaten.	One pound of tomatoes.
Was macht das zusammen?	What's the total cost?
Das kostet zwei Mark fünfzig (DM2,50).	That comes to two marks fifty.
Eine Mark zwanzig (DM1,20).	One mark twenty.
Drei Äpfel.	Three apples.
Sonst noch etwas?	Anything else?
Eine Flasche Limo.	A bottle of lemonade.
Danke.	Thank you.

Emma is buying food for a picnic.

Richard is in the market.

Find Out More

1. **Bitte sehr** – The shopkeeper says **bitte sehr** when handing you your purchases. To be polite, you can say **bitte sehr** when you hand over the money to pay.

2. **Hundert Gramm Käse** – When you buy cheese and cold cuts you ask for them in grams. You can also buy them by the slice. If you wanted six slices of salami, you would ask for **sechs Scheiben Salami.**

3. **Ein Pfund Tomaten** – When you buy fruit and salads you can ask for **ein Pfund. Ein Pfund** is 500 grams. If you want to buy vegetables or larger quantities of fruit, you'll buy them by the kilo: **ein Kilo Äpfel, bitte**.

4. **Was macht das zusammen?** – You say this if you have bought more than one thing and want to know the total cost. If you buy only one thing and want to ask the price, you say **was kostet das?** – what does it cost?

Over To You

1. Your German friends have given you this shopping list. Write down how you would ask for these things.
Example:
**2 Brötchen –
Ich möchte zwei Brötchen, bitte**.

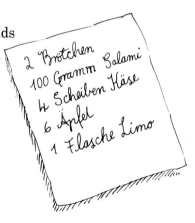

2 Brötchen
100 Gramm Salami
4 Scheiben Käse
6 Äpfel
1 Flasche Limo

2. There are eight German words hidden in this wordsearch. Can you find them and then make up a conversation to include these words?

```
P L S A L Ä M I
F I A G R P S Z
E M C R M F W Z
T O M A T E N I
T K A M I L A M
I G C M Z S T R
T G H D A N K E
B R Ö T C H E N
```

3. You are thinking about the things you want to buy for your picnic. Write down how you will ask for them in the shop.

Check your answers. Now practice reading what you have written. Then cover up some of each sentence and try to say it.

KEEPING IN TOUCH

On vacation you often want to send postcards home. You'll also need stamps. You can sometimes buy these where you buy your postcards or you can go to the post office (**die Post**). You can phone home from a public phone booth (**eine Telefonzelle**).

KEY PHRASES

Ich möchte eine Ansichtskarte.	I'd like a postcard.
Vier Ansichtskarten, bitte.	Four postcards, please.
Das macht zwei Mark, bitte.	Two marks, please.
Verkaufen Sie Briefmarken für Großbritannien?	Do you sell stamps for Great Britain?
Für eine Ansichtskarte?	For a postcard?
Für einen Brief?	For a letter?
Ich möchte nach Amerika anrufen.	I'd like to make a phone call to America.
Kann ich von hier anrufen?	Can I phone from here?
Ja. Von der Telefonzelle dort drüben.	Yes. From the phone booth (phone box) over there.
Ich möchte eine Telefonkarte.	I'd like a phone card.
Wo ist die nächste Telefonzelle?	Where is the nearest phone booth (phone box)?
Wie ist die Vorwahl von Australien?	What's the area code (dialling code) for Australia?
Null, null, sechs, eins.	Zero, zero, six, one.

Richard is buying postcards and stamps.

Emma wants to phone friends in the USA.

Find Out More

1. **Vier Briefmarken für Großbritannien** –
You may want to ask for stamps to other countries,
too. Here are some more countries in German:

Amerika	America	**Irland**	Ireland
England	England	**Frankreich**	France
Schottland	Scotland	**Kanada**	Canada
Wales	Wales	**Australien**	Australia

2. When you know the kind of stamp you want,
you can ask for that without mentioning the
country: **eine Briefmarke zu achtzig Pfennig** –
one 80-pfennig stamp. You can find information
on stamps on page 81. If you want more than one
stamp you would say, for example: **vier
Briefmarken zu 80 Pfennig** – four 80-pfennig
stamps. You add an "n" to the end of **Briefmarke**
to make it plural. You'll find this is quite common
in German: **eine Ansichtskarte**, but **vier
Ansichtskarten**. German words very rarely add
"s" to make them plural.

Over To You

1. Look at the first conversation on page 19. Try
to learn it by heart. Write it down from memory.
How much did you remember? Which parts did
you find the easiest? Now concentrate on the parts
you were unsure of.
Here is the conversation again. Write it all down
from memory.

Richard: **Ich** _____ **vier** _____ **, bitte.**
Shopkeeper: **Zwei Mark, bitte.**

Richard: _____ **Sie auch** _____?

Shopkeeper: **Für Ansichtskarten?**

Richard: **Ja.** _____ **möchte** _____
Briefmarken _____ **Großbritannien, bitte.**

2. Now use the same process to learn the second conversation.

Here is the conversation again. Write it out in full.

Emma: **Kann ich** _____ **hier nach Amerika** _____ **bitte?**

Official: **Ja. Von der** _____ **dort drüben.**

Emma: **Wie ist die** _____ **von** _____ ?

Official: **Null, null, eins.**

You can do this yourself with other dialogues to help you learn them: copy them, with some blanks, and then try to fill the blanks from memory.

3. When you are the first learning a language it's often a good idea to write down what you want to say, and to practice before you actually speak.

Imagine you're on vacation in Austria and want to send some postcards. You go to the local store. Write down what you'd need to say:

(a) Say you'd like a postcard.

(b) Ask if they sell stamps.

(c) Say the stamps are for postcards for the USA.

(d) Ask for one stamp.

GETTING AROUND

During your vacation you may well decide to visit lots of places. You might need to use public transportation to do this. Here are some phrases which will help you when you travel by train:

KEY PHRASES

Einmal nach Köln, bitte, einfach.	One one-way ticket to Cologne, please.
Zweimal nach Stuttgart, bitte, hin und zurück.	Two round-trip tickets to Stuttgart, please.
Wann fährt der nächste Zug nach Freiburg?	When does the next train leave for Freiburg?
Wann kommt er an?	When does it arrive?
Um siebzehn Uhr dreißig.	At 5:30 p.m.
Um neunzehn Uhr dreißig.	At 7:30 p.m.
Muß ich umsteigen?	Do I have to change trains?
Nein, der Zug fährt direkt nach Stuttgart.	No, the train to Stuttgart is direct.
Wann fährt ein Zug nach München?	When is there a train to Munich?
Wann möchten Sie fahren?	When do you want to travel?
Morgen früh.	Tomorrow morning.
Von welchem Gleis fährt der Zug nach Hamburg?	Which platform does the train for Hamburg leave from?

Emma and Richard are going to Stuttgart for the day by train. Emma is buying the tickets.

At the end of the day they check times of trains back to Freiburg.

Find Out More

1. The phrases on page 22 can be used for buying tickets and finding out times when traveling by bus. Look out for German bus stops: **Haltestellen**. Sometimes you see just the letter H shown as a sign.

2. In Germany and Austria the 24-hour clock is used for departure and arrival times: This means that you have to add 12 to the hour if the time is after noon. So 1 p.m. is 13:00, 8 p.m. is 20:00 and 9:45 p.m. is 21:45. To understand the time you need to know numbers up to 60 in German. Look at page 63 to help you. The minutes are translated exactly as the number shown. So if the time is 20:40, you would translate the number 20 (**zwanzig**), then put the word **Uhr,** and finally translate 40 (**vierzig**). Again, you'll need to look at page 63 to help you. Thus 20:30 = **zwanzig Uhr dreißig**; 22:45 = **zweiundzwanzig Uhr fünfundvierzig.**

Over To You

1. Look at page 63. Use your tape to listen to numbers 1–60. Can you point to them as you hear them? Play your tape again and repeat the numbers until you feel confident.

2. On your tape, listen to some train times. Which times on this page were *not* mentioned?

7:10 23:30 8:30 15:20 14:35
13:50 16:45 20:15 23:10 11:55

3. Here is a conversation in a station between you (**Du**) and a ticket clerk (**Beamter**).

Du:	Beamter:
? → Bonn	13.50
in Bonn?	16.10
1 × Bonn ←→	DM30

Here is the conversation:
Du: **Wann fährt der nächste Zug nach Bonn?**
Beamter: **Um dreizehn Uhr fünfzig.**
Du: **Und wann kommt der Zug in Bonn an?**
Beamter: **Um sechzehn Uhr zehn.**
Du: **Einmal nach Bonn, hin und zurück.**
Beamter: **Das macht dreißig Mark, bitte.**

Now write out this conversation:

Du:	Beamter:
? → Berlin	14.30
in Berlin?	16.50
1 × Berlin →	DM55

Make up some more conversations like this and practice playing both parts aloud.

SOMEWHERE TO STAY

Hotels in Germany can be quite cheap, but if you want to find really cheap accommodation you should use a youth hostel (**eine Jugendherberge**) or a campground (**ein Campingplatz**). Campgrounds in both Austria and Germany are extremely well equipped.

KEY PHRASES

Haben Sie zwei Betten frei?	Do you have two beds?
Wie lange möchten Sie bleiben?	How long do you want to stay?
Eine Nacht.	One night.
Zwei Nächte.	Two nights.
Können wir Bettwäsche entleihen?	Can we rent bed linen?
Können wir hier essen?	Can we eat here?
Ja, in der Kantine.	Yes, in the canteen.
Haben Sie Platz für ein Zelt?	Have you got room for a tent?
Für eine Woche.	For one week.
Ja, wir haben Platz frei.	Yes, we have room.
Wo sind die Toiletten und die Duschen?	Where are the restrooms (toilets) and the showers?
Gibt es hier einen Campingladen?	Is there a store in the campground?

Richard and Emma are in a youth hostel.
Emma asks if they have any room available.

Later, Richard goes camping with his German friend
Thomas. Richard asks questions at a campground.

Find Out More

1. **Können wir hier essen?** There are two verbs in this sentence. A verb is a doing word. It usually shows some action. The verbs in this sentence are **können** and **essen.** When there are two verbs in a sentence in German, the second verb always goes to the end. This means that the words are in a different order from the English equivalent. For example **Können wir hier essen?** means, word for word, "Can we here eat?" Look at **Können wir Bettwäsche entleihen?** What do you think this means word for word? It means "Can we bed linen rent?"

You will use **können** very often in German to ask questions. It is important to put your second verb at the end of the sentence. If you don't, people will find it difficult to understand what you are saying.

Can you figure out what these mean?

Können wir singen?

Können wir schwimmen?

Können wir im Restaurant essen?

Können wir Tennis spielen?

2. **Eine Nacht/zwei Nächte** – You'll need to practice the pronunciation of **Nacht** and **Nächte** with the tape. If you say them properly you'll be more easily understood.

Over To You

1. When you arrive in a youth hostel or at a campground you'll need to ask questions. Can you

ask questions about the things shown in these pictures? Write out your questions.

Example: **Wo sind die Toiletten, bitte?**

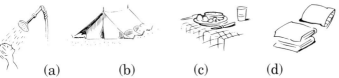

(a)　　　　(b)　　　　(c)　　　　(d)

2. Make up a phrase for each of these words.
Example: **Platz: Haben Sie Platz für ein Zelt?**

**Platz　Woche　entleihen　Kantine　lange
frei　Wo　Nächte**

3. You've arrived at a campground in Germany.
Write out this conversation in German:

You ask the owner if he has any room for a tent.

_____

He asks you how long you would like to stay.

_____

You say for two nights.

_____

He says he has room.

_____

GOING OUT

When you are staying in Germany you'll meet German people of your age. You may well want to make arrangements to meet them and go out somewhere. Here are some phrases which will help you to make such arrangements:

KEY PHRASES

Möchtest du heute nachmittag schwimmen gehen?	Would you like to go swimming this afternoon?
Möchtest du ins Kino gehen?	Would you like to go to the movies?
Möchtest du in die Stadt gehen?	Would you like to go into town?
Möchtest du zur Disko gehen?	Would you like to go to the disco?
Möchtest du ins Café gehen?	Would you like to go to the café?
Ja, gerne.	Yes, I'd like that.
Nein, danke. Ich möchte lieber ins Kino gehen.	No, thank you. I'd prefer to go to the movies.
Wo treffen wir uns?	Where shall we meet?
Vor dem Kino.	In front of the theater.
An der Bushaltestelle.	At the bus stop.
Wann treffen wir uns?	When shall we meet?
Um drei Uhr dreißig.	At three thirty.
Gut.	O.K.

Richard is arranging to go out with two German friends, Ilka and Thomas.

Emma is arranging to go out.

Find Out More

1. **Möchtest du ins Kino gehen?** – In German there is more than one word for "you." In many situations when you talk with adults you use **Sie,** but when you are talking to a friend or someone of your own age you use **du.**

Möchtest du ins Café gehen?
Möchtest du zur Disko gehen?

2. **Um drei Uhr** – To state a time to meet in German, you need to give the hour followed by the word "**Uhr**". So, "at four o'clock" would be **um vier Uhr**. "At twelve o'clock" would be **um zwölf Uhr**. If you want to meet at half past the hour, add the word for thirty: **dreißig**. So, "at three thirty" is **um drei Uhr dreißig**; "at ten thirty" is **um zehn Uhr dreißig**. See page 63 for numbers.

3. **Ich möchte lieber ins Kino gehen** – You use **ich möchte lieber** to say you prefer something. The second verb, **gehen**, comes at the end.

Over To You

1. Using these clocks, write the answers to this message. **Wann trefen wir uns?**

Example: 3:00–
Um drei Uhr

2. Thomas has left a note for Richard in code. All the vowels have been left out. Write out the message correctly.

Mchtst du ht schwmmn ghn?
Wnn trffn wr ns?
W trffn wr ns?

3. Here is a conversation about making arrangements:

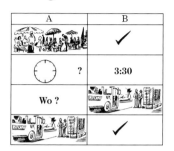

This is the conversation in full:

A: **Möchtest du ins Café gehen?**
B: **Ja, gerne.**
A: **Wann treffen wir uns?**
B: **Um drei Uhr dreißig.**
A: **Wo treffen wir uns?**
B: **An der Bushaltestelle.**
A: **An der Bushaltestelle?**
B: **Ja, an der Bushaltestelle.**

Now write out this conversation:

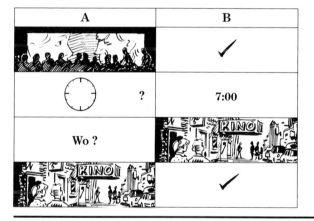

SOLVING PROBLEMS

You always hope when you are away that you'll
have no problems, but it is better to be prepared.
If you are ill in Germany or Austria the best
thing to try first is a visit to a pharmacy (**die
Apotheke**). If you are really ill you'll need to
make an appointment with a doctor (**ein Arzt**)
or a dentist (**ein Zahnarzt**). Here are some
phrases that will help you:

KEY PHRASES

Mir geht es nicht gut.	I don't feel well.
Ich möchte zum Arzt gehen.	I'd like to see a doctor.
Wo gibt es einen Zahnarzt?	Where is there a dentist?
Ich möchte einen Termin haben.	I'd like to make an appointment.
Was fehlt Ihnen?	What's the matter?
Ich habe Kopfschmerzen.	I've got a headache.
Ich habe Magenschmerzen.	I've got stomachache.
Ich habe Zahnschmerzen.	I've got toothache.
Hier ist ein Rezept.	Here's a prescription.
Nehmen Sie die Tabletten dreimal am Tag.	Take the tablets three times a day.
Haben Sie Tabletten gegen Erkältung?	Do you have tablets for a cold?
Haben Sie ein Medikament gegen Husten?	Do you have any cough medicine?

Emma has not been feeling well and goes to the pharmacy.

Richard visits the doctor.

Find Out More

1. **Haben Sie Tabletten gegen Erkältung?** In German we don't ask for tablets for a cold, but tablets *against* a cold. **Gegen** means against.

2. **Schmerzen** is the German word for "pain." A lot of illnesses end with this word:

Halsschmerzen   a sore throat
Ohrenschmerzen   earache

3. **Nehmen Sie die Tabletten dreimal am Tag** – "Take the tablets *three times a day*." The frequency can be changed by changing the number in front of **mal**:

einmal   once
zweimal   twice

4. **Arzt** = male doctor, **Ärztin** = female doctor, **Zahnarzt** = male dentist, **Zahnärztin** = female dentist.

Over To You

1. You're suffering from lots of illnesses! How would you ask for tablets for these illnesses?
Example:
Haben Sie Tabletten gegen Kopfschmerzen?

2. Here's a conversation that took place in a pharmacy. The printer has omitted the letters "s," "t," and "h." Write down the conversation correctly.

A: **Guen ag. Mir ge e nic gu.**
B: **Wa fel Inen?**
A: **Ic abe Zancmerzen. Wo gib e einen Zanarz?**
Check your answer and practice saying it.

3 (a). You are staying in Germany and are not feeling well. You phone the doctor's to make an appointment:

You say that you are not well.

_____

The receptionist asks what is wrong.

_____

You say you have a headache and stomachache.

_____

You say you would like to make an appointment.

_____

3 (b). You go to a pharmacy for some medicine:

You say that you've got a stomachache.

_____

You ask the pharmacist for tablets for a stomachache.

_____

The pharmacist tells you to take them twice a day.

_____

ANSWERS

1. Haben Sie Tabletten gegen Kopfschmerzen? Zahnschmerzen? Magenschmerzen? Ohrenschmerzen? Halsschmerzen?

2. A: Guten Tag. Mir geht es nicht gut. B: Was fehlt Ihnen?

3. (a) Mir geht es nicht gut. Was fehlt Ihnen? Ich habe Kopfschmerzen und Magenschmerzen. Ich möchte einen Termin haben.

3. (b) Guten Tag. Ich habe Magenschmerzen. Haben Sie Tabletten gegen Magenschmerzen? Ja. Nehmen Sie die Tabletten zweimal am Tag.

STAYING AT A SKI RESORT

Both Southern Germany and Austria are mountainous and have ski resorts. Austria is a particularly popular destination for ski vacations. Here are some key phrases to help you on your ski trip:

KEY PHRASES

Ich möchte eine Tageskarte für dieses Skigebiet.	I'd like a day's pass for this ski area.
Eine Halbtagskarte.	A half-day pass.
Haben Sie Ihren Skipaß mit?	Do you have your ski pass?
Ich möchte mir bitte Ski und Stöcke ausleihen.	I'd like to rent (hire) some skis and poles (ski sticks
Ich möchte mir bitte Schuhe ausleihen.	I'd like to rent (hire) some boots.
Das kostet fünfzig Schilling pro Tag.	That costs 50 Austrian schillings a day.
Ich möchte an einem Skikurs für Anfänger teilnehmen.	I'd like to take part in a ski class (course) for beginners.
Das kostet zweihundert Schilling pro Tag.	That costs 200 Austrian schillings a day.
Ich bin noch nie skigefahren.	I've never been skiing before.
Ich möchte eine Suppe.	I'd like some soup.
Eine heiße Schokolade, bitte.	A hot chocolate, please.
Gibt es ein Café in der Bergstation?	Is there a café up in the ski station?
Wie ist der Schnee heute?	What's the snow like today?
Der Schnee ist heute gut.	The snow is good today.

Richard and Emma are on a skiing weekend in Austria. Emma is going skiing.

Richard is in a ski shop.

Find Out More

1. **Ski** – This is not pronounced in the same way as it is in English. You do not hear the letter "k." Instead it sounds like the English word "she." Listen carefully when you hear the cassette.

2. **Bergstation** – There are two ski stations. The **Bergstation** is at the top of the ski lift. The **Talstation** is in the valley.

3. **Skilift**: There are various ways of getting up the mountain:

Seilbahn	cable car
Sessellift	chair lift
Schlepplift	rope tow

4. **ÖS50**: This stands for 50 Austrian schillings. The Schilling is the currency of Austria. In 1 **Schilling** there are 100 **Groschen.**

Over To You

1. Here is a bulletin board outside the ski station. Snow has covered parts of the words. Write out all the words on the board.

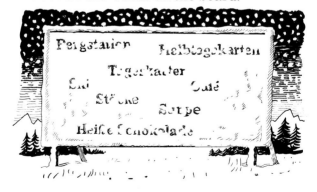

2. What do you think these people are saying?
Write down your answers.

Example: 1. **Ich möchte mir Ski und Stöcke ausleihen.**

Now check your answers and practice saying them.

BUYING DRINKS & SNACKS

Eating out in another country is fun, but it can be expensive. It is often best just to stop at a café (**ein Café**) or snack bar (**eine Imbißstube**). In a café you can buy drinks and cakes and ice cream. There you'll need to call the waiter (**Herr Ober!**) or waitress (**Fräulein!**). In a snack bar you'll buy your food at the counter. Snack bars sell hot food, too.

KEY PHRASES

Bitte sehr?	Can I help you?
Ich möchte eine Cola.	I'd like a cola.
Einen Orangensaft.	An orange juice.
Eine Tasse Tee mit Milch.	A cup of tea with milk.
Eine Tasse Kaffee.	A cup of coffee.
Ein Stück Kuchen.	A piece of cake.
Ein Eis.	An ice cream.
Einmal Bratwurst.	One serving (portion) of sausage.
Einmal Hähnchen mit Pommes.	One serving (portion) of chicken and fries (chips).
Ein Käsebrot.	One cheese sandwich.
Ein Schinkenbrot.	One ham sandwich.

Emma and Ilka are ordering some drinks in a café.

Richard and Thomas are buying food at a snack bar.

Find Out More

1. In German there are different words for "a."
You say *eine* **Tasse Tee**, but *ein* **Stück Kuchen**.
It is best to learn **ein** or **eine** when you learn the
new word, e.g. **ein Eis**, **eine Cola**.

2. When you want to order one serving of food,
you say **einmal,** e.g. **einmal Bratwurst.** If you
want two servings, you say **zweimal Bratwurst.**
How would you order *three* servings of sausage?

3. Sometimes you see on the bill the words **mit
Bedienung**. This means service is included, so
you do not need to leave a tip. Otherwise you
should leave 10% of the total cost for a tip.

Over To You

1. These people are thinking about what to
order. Write down what they would say.

Check your answers, then practice learning
them. To help you to do this, practice saying
them as you think they might be said by famous
people, e.g., Michael Jordan, Madonna, or the
President.

2. Sometimes menus are written on boards outside cafés and snack bars. The words on this menu have gotten smudged. Can you write out the menu again?

3. You are in a snack bar with your friend. You both want a hot meal and something to drink. Write out what you would say.

SHOPPING FOR PRESENTS

While you are on vacation you may want to buy some presents to take home. You'll find a good selection in stores in Germany and Austria. Here are some phrases which will help you when you go shopping.

KEY PHRASES

Ich möchte dieses T-Shirt, bitte.	I would like this T-shirt, please.
Ich habe das in Blau und Gelb.	I have that in blue and in yellow.
Ich nehme das in Gelb.	I'll take the yellow one.
Das kostet hundertfünfzig Schilling.	That costs 150 Austrian schillings.
Verkaufen Sie Pralinen?	Do you sell chocolates?
Wir haben Schachteln Pralinen zu zwanzig und zu vierzig Schilling.	We have boxes of chocolates for 20 Austrian schillings and for 40 Austrian schillings.
Ich möchte eine Schachtel zu zwanzig Schilling, bitte.	I would like a box for 20 Austrian schillings, please.
Welche Farben haben Sie?	What colors do you have?
Kann ich es anprobieren?	Can I try it on?
Ich möchte diesen Stift, bitte.	I would like this pen please.
Ich möchte diese Kassette, bitte.	I would like this cassette, please.
Ich möchte dieses Poster, bitte.	I would like this poster, please.

Richard sees a T-shirt which he wants to buy.

Guten Tag. Ich möchte dieses T-Shirt, bitte.

Ich habe das in Blau und Gelb.

Ich nehme das in Gelb, bitte.

Das kostet hundertfünfzig Schilling.

Emma is looking for a box of chocolates to take home as a present.

Guten Morgen. Verkaufen Sie Pralinen?

Ja, wir haben Schachteln zu vierzig Schilling und zu zwanzig Schilling.

Ich möchte eine Schachtel zu zwanzig Schilling, bitte.

Find Out More

1. **Ich habe das in Blau und Gelb:** In this phrase you have learned two colors in German, but you may want to talk about other colors too, or perhaps you do not like blue and yellow. Here are some other colors in German:

rot	–	red	**weiß**	–	white
grün	–	green	**schwarz**	–	black
braun	–	brown	**grau**	–	gray

2. **Dieses T-Shirt:** the word **dieses** means "this." The ending changes, depending upon whether the word following it is a **der, die** or **das** word. For **der** words you use **dieser,** for **die** words you use **diese** and for **das** words you use **dieses. T-Shirt** is a **das** word. **Schachtel** is a **die** word: **Ich möchte diese Schachtel Pralinen, bitte**.

MONEY

All the prices in the examples are in Austrian schillings. When you stay in Germany, you will see that the prices are in deutschmarks. The abbreviation for this is **DM**.

Over To You

1. Can you tell what these are?

Write out how you would ask for each item in the shop.

Example: **Ich möchte dieses Poster, bitte.**

Check your answers and practice learning them, for example, by trying to say each one ten times in 30 seconds and timing yourself.

2. From the presents in exercise one, choose two things you'd like to buy. Make up two conversations – one for each present you have chosen. Now listen to your tape. Thomas is buying presents, too. Did he choose the same presents you did?

3. You are shopping for presents. Write out this conversation in full:

Say you would like this pen.

_____

Ask what colors they have.

_____

I have it in red and green.

_____

Say you will take it in red.

_____

MAKING FRIENDS

When you are staying in Austria or Germany you'll meet people of your own age. Here are some phrases which will help you get to know them better:

KEY PHRASES

Hallo. Bleibst du auch hier in der Jugendherberge?	Hello. Are you also staying here in the youth hostel?
Ja. Wir sind auf einer Klassenfahrt.	Yes. We're on a class trip.
Wie heißt du?	What's your name?
Ich heiße . . .	My name is . . .
Woher kommst du?	Where do you come from?
Ich komme aus Deutschland.	I come from Germany.
Hast du Geschwister?	Do you have any brothers or sisters?
Ich habe eine Schwester / einen Bruder.	I've got a sister / a brother.
Wie alt bist du?	How old are you?
Ich bin vierzehn.	I'm fourteen.
Ich gehe jetzt in die Stadt.	I'm going into town now.
Möchtest du mitkommen?	Would you like to come, too?

Whilst Emma and Richard are in Austria they meet some people they would like to get to know better.

Hallo. Bleibst du hier in der Jugendherberge?

Ja. Wir sind auf einer Klassenfahrt.

Wie heißt du?

Ich heiße Ilka.

Richard has met someone called Thomas. He starts talking to him.

Wie alt bist du?

Ich bin vierzehn.

Woher kommst du?

Ich komme aus Deutschland.

Find Out More

1. **Wie heißt du?** In German there is more than one word for "you." When you talk with adults you use **Sie**, but when you talk to someone of your own age you use **du**.

Example: **Wie heißt du?**
          Ich heiße Ilka
          Wie heißen Sie?
          Ich heiße Herr Schmidt

2. **Ich komme aus Deutschland:** You use **Ich komme aus** to say which country you come from. Here are some more countries which you might need to know:

aus England	– from England
aus Irland	– from Ireland
aus Schottland	– from Scotland
aus Wales	– from Wales
aus Österreich	– from Austria
aus den USA	– from the USA
aus Kanada	– from Canada
aus Australien	– from Australia

Over To You

1. While staying in Austria you see these ads for penpals on the bulletin board.

Ich heiße Brigitte.
Ich bin dreizehn.
Ich komme aus
Salzburg in Österreich.
Ich habe einen Bruder.

Ich heiße Jörg.
Ich komme aus Dresden
in Deutschland.
Ich bin sechzehn.
Ich habe einen Bruder.

Write down what each card says in English.
Which person would you like to write to, and why?

2. Now use one of these cards to help you write
a card of your own for the bulletin board.

3. Write out this conversation. You are staying in
Austria and meet a boy who is on a school trip.

You say hello and ask the boy whether he's staying in the youth
hostel.

_____

He says yes, he's on a school trip and asks your name.

_____

You tell him your name, age, and where you come from.

_____

He says his name is Berndt and that he comes from Innsbruck
in Austria.

_____

You say you are going into town and ask if he wants to come.

_____

ANSWERS

1. (a) My name is Brigitte. I'm 13. I come from Salzburg in
Austria. I've got one brother.
(b) My name is Jörg. I come from Dresden in Germany. I'm
16. I've got one brother.

2. Hallo. Ich heiße . . . Ich bin . . .
Ich komme aus . . . Ich habe . . .

3. A: Hallo. Bleibst du hier in der Jugendherberge?
B: Ja. Ich bin auf einer Klassenfahrt. Wie heißt du?
A: Ich heiße . . .
Ich bin . . . Woher kommst du?
B: Ich heiße Berndt, ich komme aus Innsbruck in
Österreich.
A: Ich gehe in die Stadt. Möchtest du mitkommen?

VISITING A FAMILY

During your stay in Austria or Germany you'll have the opportunity to make friends. If you are lucky you may be invited to their house to have a meal with them. Here are some phrases which will help you in this situation:

KEY PHRASES

Guten Tag. Komm herein.	Hello. Come in.
Hier ist mein Vater / meine Mutter.	This is my father / my mother.
Es freut mich sehr, Sie kennenzulernen.	I'm very pleased to meet you.
Magst du Hähnchen?	Do you like chicken?
Ja, ich mag Hähnchen.	Yes, I like chicken.
Möchtest du noch etwas Suppe?	Would you like some more soup?
Nein, danke. Das war sehr gut.	No, thank you. That was very good.
Ja, bitte, aber nur ein bißchen.	Yes, please, but just a little.
Magst du Pommes Frites?	Do you like french fries (chips)?
Magst du Schwarzwälder-kirschtorte?	Do you like Black Forest cake (gateau)?
Was möchtest du gern trinken?	What would you like to drink?
Ich möchte gern eine Cola.	I would like a cola.

Richard has been invited to Thomas's house.

Emma is having lunch at Ilka's house.

Find Out More

1. **Nein, danke. Das war sehr gut** – You'd say this if you didn't want a second helping. It's a polite way of saying that you've had enough.

2. **Ich mag / ich möchte** – These two phrases have different meanings. It is important not to confuse them:

ich mag   I like
ich möchte   I'd like

3. In these phrases you have learned the German for some foods which you could be offered in a family. Here are some more for you to learn:

Melone	melon
Schnitzel	a pork or veal steak
Kartoffeln	potatoes
Salat	salad
Käse	cheese
Eis	ice cream

Over To You

1. Write out this conversation in full. You have been invited to have lunch with a German family.

The mother greets you and asks you to come in.

_____

Your friend introduces you to his mother.

_____

You say you are very pleased to meet her.

_____

2. Which of these foods do you like? If you like them, accept a second helping, e.g.: **Ja, bitte, aber nur ein bißchen**. If you do not want a second helping, say so politely: **Nein, danke. Das war sehr gut**.

3. Here is another conversation to write down. This time you're having a meal with an Austrian family.

Your friend asks if you would like some more soup.

_____

You say you would like a little.

_____

Your friend asks if you like chicken and french fries.

_____

You say you do, very much.

_____

USEFUL WORDS AND PHRASES

In this section you'll find additional words and phrases
linked to the twelve **Themen**. You'll also find a list of days
and months, and phrases about the weather.

THEMA 1 – ASKING THE WAY

das Kino	the movie theater
die Bank	the bank
die Kirche	the church
das Hotel	the hotel
das Restaurant	the restaurant
der Marktplatz	the market place
der Sportplatz	the sports ground
der Park	the park
über die Brücke	over the bridge
über die Kreuzung	across the intersection
um die Ecke	around the corner
zwischen der Post und dem Verkehrsamt	between the post office and the information office

THEMA 2 – SHOPPING FOR FOOD

Wurst	sausage
Schinken	ham
Butter	butter
Zucker	sugar
Eier	eggs
Kekse	cookies
Birnen	pears
Äpfel	apples
Orangen	oranges
Bananen	bananas
Pfirsiche	peaches
Erdbeeren	strawberries
Trauben	grapes
eine Gurke	a cucumber
Kopfsalat	lettuce
Orangensaft	orange juice
Apfelsaft	apple juice
Bier	beer
Milch	milk

THEMA 3 – KEEPING IN TOUCH

Ich möchte einen Stift, bitte.	I'd like a pen, please.
Ich möchte ein Paket nach Kanada schicken.	I'd like to send a package to Canada.

THEMA 4 – GETTING AROUND

Wann fährt der nächste Bus zur Stadtmitte, bitte?	When does the next bus go downtown?
Wie oft fährt ein Bus nach Freiburg?	How often do buses go to Freiburg?
Alle dreißig Minuten.	Every half hour.
Bushaltestelle	bus stop
Wann kommt der Zug in Kiel an?	When does the train arrive in Kiel?
Ich möchte einen Platz reservieren.	I'd like to reserve a seat.
Nichtraucher	non-smoking
Raucher	smoking
Abfahrt	departure
Ankunft	arrival
Ist dieser Platz frei?	Is this seat free?
besetzt	occupied, taken

THEMA 5 – SOMEWHERE TO STAY

Familienname	last name
Vorname	first name
Adresse	address
Geburtsdatum	date of birth
Geburtsort	place of birth
Staatsangehörigkeit	nationality
Schlüssel	key
Ich habe einen Platz reserviert.	I've reserved a place.
da drüben	over there
unter den Bäumen	under the trees
neben dem Fluß	near the river
am See	near the lake
im Schatten	in the shade
Können Sie dieses Formular bitte ausfüllen?	Can you fill out this form, please?

Anmeldung	reception
Zimmernachweis	information about accommodation
Zimmer frei	rooms available
Haben Sie ein Zimmer für heute nacht?	Do you have a room for tonight?
ein Einzelzimmer	a single room
ein Doppelzimmer	a double room
mit Bad	with bath
Ist der Preis inklusive Frühstück?	Does the price include breakfast?

THEMA 6 – GOING OUT

Hast du heute abend etwas vor?	Are you doing anything this evening?
Möchtest du schwimmen gehen?	Would you like to go swimming?
heute morgen	this morning
heute nachmittag	this afternoon
morgen	tomorrow
morgen früh	tomorrow morning
morgen abend	tomorrow evening
bis heute abend	see you this evening

THEMA 7 – SOLVING PROBLEMS

Mein Arm tut weh.	My arm hurts.
mein Fuß	my foot
mein Bein	my leg
mein Rücken	my back
mein Auge	my eye
mein Mund	my mouth
meine Hand	my hand
mein Knie	my knee
mein Knöchel	my ankle
Ich habe Fieber.	I've got a fever.
Ich habe einen Sonnenbrand.	I've got sunburn.
Ich habe Durchfall.	I've got diarrhea.
Ich habe Verstopfung.	I'm constipated.
Mir ist übel.	I feel sick.
Ich habe einen Mückenstich.	I've got an insect bite.

THEMA 8 – STAYING IN A SKI RESORT

Ich möchte schlittschuhlaufen.   I'd like to go skating.

Ich möchte rodeln.   I'd like to go tobogganing.

THEMA 9 – BUYING DRINKS AND SNACKS

Salamibrot	salami sandwich
Mineralwasser	mineral water
Weißwein	white wine
Rotwein	red wine
Mayonnaise	mayonnaise
Senf	mustard
Ketchup	ketchup
Frikadelle	a type of hamburger
Bratwurst	fried sausage
Zwiebelwurst	onion sausage
Bockwurst	pork and beef sausage, cooked in boiling water
Schaschlik	kebab
Apfelkuchen	apple cake
ein Kännchen Kaffee	a pot of coffee
heiße Schokolade	hot chocolate
eine Tasse Tee	a cup of tea
mit Milch	with milk
mit Zitrone	with lemon
mit Schlagsahne	with whipped cream
ohne Schlagsahne	without whipped cream
Herr Ober!	Waiter!
Fräulein!	Waitress!
Zahlen, bitte	The bill, please.
die Speisekarte, bitte	The menu, please.
Suppe	soup
Melone	melon
Krabbencocktail	shrimp cocktail
grüner Salat	green salad
gemischter Salat	mixed salad
Gurkensalat	cucumber salad
Tomatensalat	tomato salad
Forelle	trout
Entchen	duck
Kartoffeln	potatoes
Erbsen	peas
Karotten	carrots
Blumenkohl	cauliflower

grüne Bohnen	green beans
Eis	ice-cream
Erdbeereis	strawberry ice-cream
Schokoladeneis	chocolate ice-cream
Zitroneneis	lemon ice-cream
Vanilleeis	vanilla ice-cream
Was ist das?	What's that?

THEMA 10 – SHOPPING FOR PRESENTS

dieses Buch	this book
dieses Sweatshirt	this sweatshirt
diesen Fußball	this football
diese Sonnenbrille	these sunglasses
diese Tasche	this bag
diesen Pulli	this pullover
diese Schuhe	these shoes
diese Socken	these socks
Das ist mir zu teuer.	It's too expensive.
Das ist mir zu groß.	It's too big.
Das ist mir zu klein.	It's too small.
Das ist mir zu lang.	It's too long.
Das ist mir zu kurz.	It's too short.
Soll ich das als Geschenk einpacken?	Should I gift-wrap it?

THEMA 11 – MAKING FRIENDS

Das liegt im Norden	It's in the north
im Süden / im Westen / im Osten.	in the south / in the west / in the east.
Ich bin ein Einzelkind.	I'm an only child.
Ich habe einen Hund.	I've got a dog.
Ich habe eine Katze.	I've got a cat.
Ich habe ein Pferd.	I've got a horse.
Ich schwimme gern.	I like swimming.
Was machst du gern?	What do you like doing?
Ich spiele gern Fußball.	I like playing football.
Ich spiele gern Tennis.	I like playing tennis.
Ich fahre gern Rad.	I like cycling.
Ich sehe gern fern.	I like watching television.
Ich reite gern.	I like riding horses.
Das mag ich sehr.	I like that a lot.
Das mag ich nicht.	I don't like that.
Das finde ich echt super.	I think that's great.

THEMA 12 – VISITING A FAMILY

Frühstück	breakfast
Mittagessen	lunch
Abendessen	evening meal

NUMBERS

It will help you in many situations if you can understand and use numbers. Here are the numbers you'll need. Practice them with your cassette. Try to repeat them and learn them in groups.

1	eins	36	sechsunddreißig
2	zwei	37	siebenunddreißig
3	drei	38	achtunddreißig
4	vier	39	neununddreißig
5	fünf	40	vierzig
6	sechs	41	einundvierzig
7	sieben	42	zweiundvierzig
8	acht	43	dreiundvierzig
9	neun	44	vierundvierzig
10	zehn	45	fünfundvierzig
11	elf	46	sechsundvierzig
12	zwölf	47	siebenundvierzig
13	dreizehn	48	achtundvierzig
14	vierzehn	49	neunundvierzig
15	fünfzehn	50	fünfzig
16	sechzehn	51	einundfünfzig
17	siebzehn	52	zweiundfünfzig
18	achtzehn	53	dreiundfünfzig
19	neunzehn	54	vierundfünfzig
20	zwanzig	55	fünfundfünfzig
21	einundzwanzig	56	sechsundfünfzig
22	zweiundzwanzig	57	siebenundfünfzig
23	dreiundzwanzig	58	achtundfünfzig
24	vierundzwanzig	59	neunundfünfzig
25	fünfundzwanzig	60	sechzig
26	sechsundzwanzig	61	einundsechzig
27	siebenundzwanzig	62	zweiundsechzig
28	achtundzwanzig	63	dreiundsechzig
29	neunundzwanzig	64	vierundsechzig
30	dreißig	65	fünfundsechzig
31	einunddreißig	66	sechsundsechzig
32	zweiunddreißig	67	siebenundsechzig
33	dreiunddreißig	68	achtundsechzig
34	vierunddreißig	69	neunundsechzig
35	fünfunddreißig	70	siebzig

71	einundsiebzig	87	siebenundachtzig
72	zweiundsiebzig	88	achtundachtzig
73	dreiundsiebzig	89	neunundachtzig
74	vierundsiebzig	90	neunzig
75	fünfundsiebzig	91	einundneunzig
76	sechsundsiebzig	92	zweiundneunzig
77	siebenundsiebzig	93	dreiundneunzig
78	achtundsiebzig	94	vierundneunzig
79	neunundsiebzig	95	fünfundneunzig
80	achtzig	96	sechsundneunzig
81	einundachtzig	97	siebenundneunzig
82	zweiundachtzig	98	achtundneunzig
83	dreiundachtzig	99	neunundneunzig
84	vierundachtzig	100	hundert
85	fünfundachtzig	150	hundertfünfzig
86	sechsundachtzig	200	zweihundert

DAYS

Sonntag	Sunday	**Donnerstag**	Thursday
Montag	Monday	**Freitag**	Friday
Dienstag	Tuesday	**Samstag**	Saturday
Mittwoch	Wednesday		

MONTHS

Januar	January	**Mai**	May	**September**	September
Februar	February	**Juni**	June	**Oktober**	October
März	March	**Juli**	July	**November**	November
April	April	**August**	August	**Dezember**	December

THE WEATHER

Wie ist das Wetter?	What's the weather like?
Es regnet.	It's raining.
Es schneit.	It's snowing.
Es ist kalt.	It's cold.
Es ist heiß.	It's hot.
Es ist wolkig.	It's cloudy.
Die Sonne scheint.	It's sunny.

GERMANY
AND
AUSTRIA

VISITING GERMANY AND AUSTRIA

So you want to visit Germany or Austria?

Where are these countries exactly?

Here is a map which shows you. Look at the countries / states which surround Germany and Austria.

Germany is the largest country in the European Community. Compare its size with that of your country.

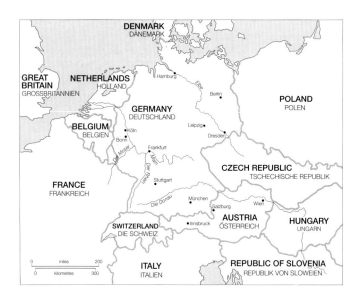

HIER IST DEUTSCHLAND

Germany is a country of great variety. It has large international cities where you can buy anything and where life is fast and fun. It also has quiet little villages in beautiful countryside.

In the North there are the seaside resorts. These are good for healthy vacations, for windsurfing and sports. In the South there are the Alps. Here you will find many popular ski resorts.

Germany is a country for young people. There is plenty to do and plenty to see. Until 1989 Berlin was a divided city, separated by the Berlin wall into East and West Berlin. Now it is the capital of Germany.

Berlin is a city full of fun, especially in the summertime. Everywhere you can see people sitting in street cafés, perhaps watching street performers, fire-eaters, skateboarders or musicians. The **Kurfürstendamm**, Berlin's longest street, is where you find the big hotels and the expensive stores, **Virgin** and **Fnac** – they sell everything!

You can even swim in Berlin in the **Wannsee** (Lake Wannsee) – and it is often hot enough to do so. Berlin is a popular place for young people. Go there if you can.

Some Places To Visit

**For those who like sports –
Kiel and the North Frisian Islands**

Kiel lies on the **Ostee** – the Baltic Sea. It is famous for its yacht races. Every June there is Kiel week, a meeting point for the world's best yachtspeople. This regatta attracts everything from tall ships to dinghies.

To the northeast of Kiel, in the **Nordsee** – North Sea – are the North Frisian Islands. They are some of Germany's few seaside resorts. Although the climate is not guaranteed to give you a suntan, there is plenty to do. The area is ideal for yachting and windsurfing, and if you enjoy cycling or riding horses then the kilometers and kilometers of flat coastline give you perfect conditions for these sports. If you enjoy outdoor activities, this could be just the place for you.

The Rhine and the Moselle

The rivers Rhine and Moselle (in German **der Rhein** and **die Mosel**) are very popular places for school trips. There are lots of hotels and youth hostels, and school parties are well-catered to. They are also in the center of Germany and therefore easier to get to. If you live in the USA or Canada, there are airports near the major Rhine resorts that handle international flights.

The Rhine flows from the north to the south of Germany. The most popular stretch of river for vacationers is between Mainz and Bonn.

Here you can stay in small towns where you can find your way around easily and practice your German. There are also several larger towns on the Rhine for day trips:

- Köln – in English we say Cologne – is famous for its cathedral and has good shops.
- Bonn was until recently the capital of West Germany. It is also the birthplace of Beethoven and you can visit his small house in the old part of the town.

All along the Rhine you can visit old castles – there are more than 30 of them. As you walk up the hillside to visit a castle you'll see the famous vineyards of the Rhine. The Rhine valley is a major wine growing area of Europe.
The Moselle is a tributary of the Rhine and equally popular with visitors. One good way of seeing the Rhine and the Moselle is to take a trip on a Rhine steamer.

München (Munich)

Munich (**München** in German) is the capital of Bavaria – a region in South Germany. It is a lively city and has everything for young people. In fact it produces a tourist guide especially for young people. This guide not only tells you all about the exciting things in Munich, it also gives you lots of information on such things as eating and drinking, shopping, cheap travel and cheap accommodation. It has a section of practical advice to help you when you are away from home. If you would like one of these brochures you should write to:

Tourist Office of the City of Munich,
D-8000 München 1,
Germany.

The brochure is called "Young People's Guide to Munich" and is written in English.

In the old part of Munich there are shops in beautiful pedestrian precincts with fountains, as well as a cathedral, a castle and remnants of the

city walls. You must visit the famous Olympic park and village with its 270-meter Olympic tower and stadiums. This was the site of the Olympic Games in 1972, and entry is free.

If you like music and entertainment, you'll find plenty of variety, including classical, rock and pop concerts. Sometimes these are in the open air in the parks. The parks are also a meeting place for young people. There you can find shade from the heat of the sun or, if you prefer, you can go boating on the lake.

In July, Munich has its opera festival and in September/October there is the marathon 16-day **Oktoberfest** (Beer Festival). There is always something to do in Munich!

Schwarzwald (Black Forest)

This vast area of pine forest is in South Germany near the Alps. The capital city of the Black Forest is Freiburg. It lies on the **Dreiländereck**, the frontier of three countries – Germany, France and Switzerland. The city has a wonderful cathedral and attractive narrow streets with small streams. The houses have steep roofs to cope with the heavy snow in winter. This is a resort area all year. In the summer you can swim in the lakes. In the autumn and spring you can walk for miles in the forests.

In the winter the whole area is covered in deep snow. There are many ski resorts and as you walk through the forest you'll be able to stand at the top of ski jumps and look down into the valley below.

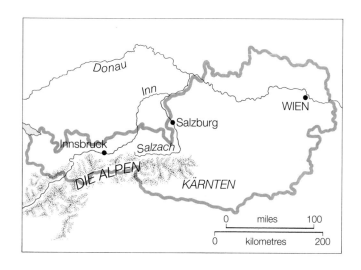

HIER IST ÖSTERREICH

When you learn German you can also make yourself understood in Austria. German is spoken by everybody here, even if the dialect sometimes takes a bit of getting used to!

Austria is a wonderful country filled with mountains and lakes. It is one of the major countries of Europe for skiing vacations. There is also plenty to do in the summer, from just lazing around sunbathing to almost any sport you could wish to try. Have you ever tried water-skiing, para-gliding or windsurfing? All these are popular sports on Austrian lakes.

Some Places to Visit

Wien (Vienna)

Vienna (**Wien** in German) is the capital of Austria. It is a city of beautiful buildings, palaces, and gardens. Two of the most beautiful palaces are Schönbrunn Palace and the Belvedere. The city also boasts a world-famous chocolate cake, the **Sachertorte** – delicious but very expensive! Try some in one of the many Viennese coffee houses.

Vienna is a capital of music. Many famous composers have lived here, including Mozart, Haydn, Beethoven, Schubert, Brahms and Strauss, and it is of course the home of the Viennese waltz.

For young people there is the Prater, Vienna's amusement park, founded in 1766. Shopping in Vienna can be fun, too. Try looking in the flea market where you can find some low-priced items, but look at the price tags carefully, as there are also some very expensive presents here.

Innsbruck

Home of the Winter Olympics in 1964 and 1976, this is the city for all winter sports. You can ski here in winter and even in summer on the glaciers.

In the old part of the city there are covered shopping arcades. In this area you will see a famous old house with a gold roof. The whole of the old city is very picturesque. Don't forget your camera!

If you go to Innsbruck you should also take the opportunity to go on the funicular railway to the top of the Hungerburg hill. From here you will have an excellent view of the city.

Salzburg

This is the birthplace of Mozart and probably the most beautiful city in Austria. It is situated in the mountains, with a wide river and attractive old buildings. There are busy shopping streets such as the famous Getreidegasse and large cool squares where young people gather together.

Above the city is a castle – Festung Hohensalzburg. You can either walk up to this or, if you are feeling less energetic, you can pay and go on the funicular railway and walk back to the Mönchsberg hill where an elevator will take you down to the city again.

Kärnten (Carinthia)

Carinthia (**Kärnten** in German) is the Austrian lake district. The scenery is spectacular. There are high mountains and large lakes. Some of the lakes are fed by thermal springs. **Ossiachersee**, one of these lakes, stays at a constant temperature of 29°C (84°F) in the summer. Here swimming is a real pleasure, as are other water sports.

There are lots of campgrounds in this area. They are all equipped to a high standard and are, of course, cheap places to stay and a good place to meet young Austrians and Germans.

Quiz

Look at these words.

Kärnten · **Schönbrunn** · **1972 Olympics** · **Wine**
Virgin Kurfürstendamm · **Bonn** · **Warm lakes**
Lake Wannsee · **Castles** · **Beer Festival** · **Strauss**
Lake district · **Prater** · **Vineyards** · **München**
Sachertorte · **Capital of Bavaria**

Which places would you connect them with? Try to list them under these place names:

Rhine   Berlin   Munich   Vienna   Carinthia

For example, if you think that Bonn has a connection with the Rhine, write Bonn under Rhine.

OUT AND ABOUT

The first part of this book contains twelve
Themen, or themes, designed to help you in
different situations. This second part of the book
will give you practical information and tips to
help you to get more out of these situations.

Thema 1: Asking the Way

German and Austrian towns are usually well
marked with signs. It will save you some time if
you learn to understand some of them.

As you enter a
town, you will
often see this sign.

This shows you the way to the town center.
Here are some other signs which you should
understand.

Some of these you will perhaps understand already or be able to guess. Here is the English for each of the signs:

Information	
Auskunft	information
Verkehrsamt	
Bahnhof	station
Parkplatz	parking lot
Marktplatz	market place
Jugendherberge	youth hostel
Zum See	to the lake
Campingplatz	campground

Crossing the Road

When you're in a strange town and trying to find your way, it's very important to take care crossing the street.

- Only cross at a pedestrian crossing.

- Only cross when you can see the green light.

- Traffic will stop for you if you follow this code.

- It is illegal to cross when the light is red, and police in both Austria and Germany can fine you on the spot.

Thema 2: Shopping for Food

In the larger towns in Germany stores do not close at lunch time. Generally stores are open from 9:00 a.m. to 6:00 p.m.
Smaller shops will often close for lunch and for more than an hour. You might well find them closed from 12:30 to 3:00 p.m.

On Saturdays shops are only open in the mornings, so don't leave your last-minute shopping until Saturday afternoon. Shops close at 1 o'clock on Saturdays.

On the first Saturday of each month the large stores are open all day.

In Austria shops open earlier – on Monday to Friday, they open at 8:00 a.m. and close at 6:30 p.m., but they do take a lunch break, so don't plan to shop for about two hours after noon.

On Saturdays shops close at noon.

You will often see store hours displayed on the store's entrance.

This sign tells us that the shop is open from 9 in the morning until 6 in the evening.

Currencies

- In Germany the currency is the **Deutsche Mark** (deutschmark), abbreviated to **DM**.
- In 1 **Deutsche Mark** there are 100 **Pfennige** (pfennigs). Prices are displayed on most items. If you see a price of **DM2,50**, it means that that item costs 2 marks 50 pfennigs.
- Austrian currency is the **Schilling** (schilling).
- There are 100 **Groschen** (groschen) in one **Schilling**.
- The abbreviation for the **Schilling** is **ÖS**.

If you want to buy some tomatoes and see this sign on the stall,

you will be paying 12 **Schilling** 50 **Groschen** for a pound of tomatoes.

When you are shopping for food, you'll probably be buying things for your picnic. The easiest place to shop is the supermarket. Here you'll be able to choose the foods you want. Cold meats and cheeses will be sold at a separate counter, as will fruit, and you will need to ask for them.

In both Austria and Germany you will find
SPAR shops. This is the name of a chain of
supermarkets. The German word **sparen** means
"to save."

- **Das Lebensmittelgeschäft** – In smaller
  villages this is a general store which sells
  everything.
- **Die Metzgerei** – the butcher's. Germany and
  Austria are famous for their cold meats. There
  are well over a hundred varieties!
- **Die Bäckerei** – the baker's. You'll find an
  amazing variety of bread here, from black
  bread (**Schwarzbrot**) to bread rolls
  (**Brötchen**).
- **Die Konditorei** – if you have a sweet tooth, go
  to this shop. You'll find a wonderful selection
  of cakes. Try **Erdbeertorte** – a strawberry
  tart.

Another good place to shop is the market. Here
you can see easily what everything costs. As well
as fruit stalls you'll find cheese, meat and bread
stalls. In fact you'll be able to buy everything you
want for a picnic and enjoy the atmosphere as
well.

Thema 3: Keeping in Touch

Post Offices *(Opening Hours)*

- Post offices in Germany are open from 8:00 a.m. to 4:00 p.m. Some smaller post offices close for lunch.
- In Austria, post offices are generally open from 8:00 a.m. to 12 noon and from 2:00 p.m. until 6:00 p.m.
- In some large cities, train station post offices are open 24 hours a day, including weekends and public holidays.

Sending Mail Home

Stamps from Austria:
To European countries – **ÖS6** for a postcard, **ÖS7** for a letter.
To the USA, Canada, Australia and New Zealand – **ÖS7** for a postcard, **ÖS10** for a letter.

Stamps from Germany:
To European countries – **60 Pfennig** for a postcard, **DM1** for a letter.
To the USA, Canada, Australia and New Zealand – **80 Pfennig** for a postcard, **DM1,40** for a letter.

- You don't always need to go to a post office to buy stamps. You can usually buy them in the same store where you buy your postcards.
- Mail boxes in Germany and Austria are yellow. You will be able to read the time of the next collection on the box.

Making a Phone Call

You can make a phone call from any post office or from public phone booths.

- To make a call to a foreign country you need to use the international country code, before the normal area code for the city or town. For example, the area code for Manhattan in New York City is 212. To dial this number from Germany or Austria, you will dial 001 for the USA, and then 212 for the area code for Manhattan.
- The cheapest time to phone is between 6 p.m. and 8 a.m.
- Some international country codes are:

Australia – 0061	Ireland – 010 353
Canada – 010 1	New Zealand – 0064
Great Britain – 0044	USA – 001

Thema 4: Getting Around

Seeing Germany and Austria by Train

Don't miss out on cheap ways of traveling by train if you're a student.

- **Europass**
  Valid: 1 month (Can only be bought by non-European residents; covers fifteen European countries)
  Cost: **DM960**
  Age limit: 26

- **Inter-Rail Card**
  Entitles you to 50% reduction
  Valid: 1 month
  Cost: **DM510**
  Age limit: 26
- **Flexipass**
  Valid: 5 days, 7 days, 10 days or 15 days
  Cost: **DM414, DM475, DM656** or **DM892**
  Age limit: 26
- **Tramper Monatsticket**
  Valid: 1 month
  Cost: **DM350**
  Age limit: 22 (26 for students)
- **Euro Domino Youth Pass**
  Valid: 3 days, 5 days or 10 days; 5 days only in
  Austria
  Cost: **DM223, DM247/ÖS1050** or **DM372**
  Age limit: 26
- **Rabbit Card**
  Available in Austria.
  Allows unlimited travel
  on any four days during
  a ten-day period
  Cost: **ÖS660**
  Age limit: any age

In towns the best way of getting about is by bus or
tram. Larger cities have an **U-Bahn**
(underground) or **S-Bahn** (above-ground)
railway network. You'll need to buy either an
Einzelfahrschein (one-way ticket) or a
Rückfahrschein (round-trip ticket). It is often
cheaper and more convenient to buy a book of
tickets – **Sammelkarten**.

Public Transportation in Munich

Munich has buses, trams, subways, and local trains – the **S-Bahn**. Tickets are usually bought from a machine, but you need to know the different types of tickets! This applies to other cities, too.

- The 24-hour ticket. This can be used on all four types of public transportation. All you need to do is sign it and cancel it when you begin your first trip. It is then good for 24 hours.
- Strip tickets (**Streifenkarten**). A blue strip ticket has ten strips. A trip within the city costs two strips.
- One-way ticket (**Einzelfahrschein**).
- Red children's strip ticket (**Kinderstreifenkarte**). You can only use this if you are under 15.
- **IMPORTANT – NEVER TRAVEL WITHOUT A VALID TICKET. YOU CAN BE FINED ON THE SPOT.**

Thema 5: Somewhere to Stay

So you want somewhere to stay?

In both Austria and Germany there are many youth hostels and campgrounds. They are often in extremely beautiful locations and all have good facilities. They are also cheap.

Youth Hostels

Youth hostels are very popular. It is not a good idea to arrive too late. If you want to be fairly sure of getting accommodations, you should try to check in during the afternoon.

You will need a Youth Hostel Identification Card. Either bring one with you from home or buy one in Austria or Germany. You will usually find it cheaper to buy at home, so come prepared!

In all youth hostels you can rent bed linen.

For further information on youth hostels in Germany write to either:
Deutsches Jugendherbergswerk, Postfach 220, 4930 Detmold, Germany
or: Deutsche Zentrale für Tourismus e.V., D-6000 Frankfurt am Main, Beethovenstraße 69, Germany

For information on youth hostels in Austria write to:
Österreichischer Jugendherbergsverband, Hauptverband und Travel Service, Schottenring 28, A-1010 Wien, Austria

Campgrounds

Camping is extremely popular in both Austria and Germany.

Campgrounds are good places to meet young people. You'll find campgrounds in a variety of places, from the outskirts of large cities in Germany to the shores of quiet Austrian lakes.

Write to the following address for a list of recommended campgrounds:
Deutsche Zentrale für Tourismus e.V.,
D-6000 Frankfurt am Main,
Beethovenstraße 69,
Germany

If you want to camp in Austria you should write to:
Österreichischer Campingclub,
Strandbadstraße,
A-3400 Klosterneuburg,
Austria

You can write in English or use the model letter on page 87 to ask for information about camping in a particular area. The letter asks for information about campgrounds in Munich (München). That word has been underlined. You can replace it with the name of any place you wish.

Just so that you are sure that you know what
you've written, here is a translation of the letter:

Dear Sir:

I would like information about campgrounds in Munich. Could
you please send me a list of campgrounds in the area and
enclose a list of prices.

I look forward to hearing from you.

Sincerely,

Finally, here are some signs that you might
need to understand:

Showers   *Toilets*

Entrance

Ladies   *Men*

Exit

Reception

Thema 6: Going Out

In most towns you'll probably recognize the titles of many movies that are playing. If a movie is American or British, it will generally have been dubbed into German. Sometimes films are in English with German subtitles (**Untertitel**).

There are two main television channels in Germany (**ARD** and **ZDF**) and two in Austria (**FS1** and **FS2**) – as well as regional channels and satellite television. These are some of the types of programs you may see advertised: **Sportschau** – sports news, **Tagesschau** – the news, **Filme** – films, **Abenteuerfilm** – adventure film, **Spionagethriller** – spy thriller, **Komödie** – comedy.

All German and Austrian towns have good sports facilities. Look out for signs such as: **HALLENBAD** – indoor pool, **FREIBAD** – outdoor pool, **SPORTZENTRUM** – sports center, **TENNISPLÄTZE** – tennis courts.

A visit to **Phantasialand** is a must if you are staying near the Rhine. It is located between the cities of Cologne and Bonn, just south of Brühl. It is one of Europe's leading amusement parks. It has:

- Over 26 rides and adventure shows
- The Grand Canyon train
- The Space Center – the world's largest indoor railway, taking you through space into the future
- Wild water ride
- Ghost rickshaw and many other attractions.

Thema 7: Solving Problems

It goes without saying that the best way to solve problems of illness when abroad is to avoid them. Eat sensibly and don't get too much sun.

If you are ill, however, you should try the pharmacy first **(die Apotheke).** Pharmacists in Austria and Germany are used to advising people on what medicines to take for common illnesses. But if you are really ill, you will need to see a doctor or a dentist.

It is essential that you take out health insurance for this before you travel abroad.

It's also a good idea to take out general insurance against accidents, loss and theft. You can do this through your local travel agent, but first check with your insurance carrier to see if you'll be covered while abroad. If you have to pay for a visit to the doctor, a hospital, or for medicine, be sure to get a receipt. Keep this so that you can make a claim on your return.

If you visit the dentist in either Austria or Germany you must also get a receipt so that you can present this when you make your claim.

Thema 8: Staying at a Ski Resort

You can ski in South Germany and in many parts of Austria. In all mountain areas of Austria you can ski in the winter and sometimes in the summer, too, on glaciers.

Skiing is the national sport of Austria, and the winter season lasts from the end of November to April, depending on snow conditions.

Some of the best known ski resorts are Igls, Kitzbühel, Mayrhofen, Obergurgl, St. Anton, St. Johann in Tirol and Seefeld. You can also ski (often at cheaper prices) in Styria, Lower Austria and Carinthia.

Not only is skiing excellent in Austria, there are plenty of "après-ski" activities in the evenings, too. These are as much fun as the skiing.

If you are not too keen on downhill skiing, try cross-country skiing instead. In Austria there are 16,093 kilometers of prepared trails. Equipment

for this can be rented cheaply. Trails are color-coded according to difficulty:

blue – easy
red – moderately difficult
black – difficult.

Other winter sports you may want to try are:
● disco on ice
● tobogganing
● bobsledding

When choosing a place to stay for skiing, you may find symbols in the brochure to show which facilities are available.

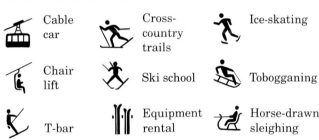

Cable car	Cross-country trails	Ice-skating
Chair lift	Ski school	Tobogganing
T-bar	Equipment rental	Horse-drawn sleighing

Thema 9: Drinks and Snacks

Food in Germany and Austria is both filling and delicious. There are many regional specialities, but on most menus you'll find different types of **Schnitzel**. **Schnitzel** is basically a pork or veal steak. It can be cooked in a variety of ways:

Wiener Schnitzel – coated in egg and breadcrumbs and fried.
Naturschnitzel – this is completely plain.

Pariserschnitzel – coated in egg and flour and fried.

Jägerschnitzel – cooked in a mushroom sauce.

Zigeunerschnitzel – cooked in a sauce with peppers and onions.

Holsteinschnitzel – like **Wiener Schnitzel** but with a fried egg on top.

Where can you eat cheaply?

- In the youth hostel.
- At an **Imbißstube** or **Schnellimbiß** – both of these are stand-up snack bars.

- At a snack bar in a department store such as Hertie.
- At small restaurants called **Gaststätte** – look for **das Menü** – the daily specials.

Kaffee und Kuchen

Cafés are generally expensive, but the selection of cakes is mouth-watering. Maybe you'll be able to treat yourself once to a coffee and cake.

Cakes to look out for are:

- **Käsesahnetorte** – a creamy cheese cake
- **Erdbeertorte** – strawberry tart
- **Obsttorte** – fruit tart
- **Schwarzwälderkirschtorte** – Black Forest cherry torte
- **Sachertorte** – dark chocolate cake
- **Apfelstrudel** – apples cooked in a fine pastry

In Germany and Austria when you order a slice of cake you'll be asked **"mit oder ohne?"** – this means "with or without?" What it is referring to is whether you want the cake with or without whipped cream.

In Germany and Austria, if you want whipped cream, you say **"Ja, mit Schlagsahne, bitte."** If you don't want cream, you simply say, **"Ohne Schlagsahne, bitte."** In Austria the word **Schlagobers** is often used instead of **Schlagsahne** to translate "whipped cream."

If you don't want coffee with your cake, you can ask for tea. This is usually served in a glass with lemon. If you want it with milk, you will have to ask for **"Tee mit Milch, bitte."**

You can also order fruit juices. Try **Apfelsaft** (apple juice), **Johannisbeersaft** (blackcurrant juice) or **Traubensaft** (grape juice).

Service is usually included on the bill. If service is included you will see the words **inklusive Bedienung** or **mit Bedienung** on the bill. If there is no service charge, it is usual to leave a 10% tip.

Quiz

Can you complete the following definitions?
1. **Holsteinschnitzel** is _____
2. **Das Menü** is _____
3. **Erdbeertorte** is _____
4. **Johannisbeersaft** is _____
5. **Apfelstrudel** is _____
6. **Schlagsahne** is _____
7. **Jägerschnitzel** is _____
8. **Schlagobers** is _____

Thema 10: Shopping for Presents

There are plenty of souvenir shops all over Germany and Austria. Do ask the price before making a decision. There are some restrictions on what you can bring back home.

- If you are under 21, you cannot buy alcohol as a present, because you won't clear U.S. customs.
- You are also not allowed to bring the following through customs:
  - flowers
  - fruit
  - vegetables
  - meats

In many shops they will gift-wrap what you buy, if you ask them. You need to say:

Könnten Sie das bitte als Geschenk einpacken?

Sometimes it can make your shopping quicker and more efficient if you understand signs in shops. Here are some signs you may see:

Special of the week

Open

Special offer

Closed

REISEANDENKEN

Souvenirs

selbstbedienung

Self-service

Thema 11: Making Friends

When you are staying in Germany you might have the opportunity to visit a German school.
- The German school day starts at 8:00 a.m.
- Pupils only go to school in the morning.
- Pupils wear no school uniform.
- All pupils learn a foreign language.
- Pupils either bring sandwiches from home or buy them from the caretaker to eat at break.
- Pupils have to take tests – **Klassenarbeiten** – in all subjects throughout the year. In each subject there are six tests a year. Subjects are marked on a 1 to 6 scale, 1 being the highest grade. If pupils get a 5 or a 6, they have failed.
- If they fail in two or more subjects, they have to repeat the year and stay in the same class.

Thema 12: Visiting a Family

Remember that when you say hello to people, especially adults, it is polite to shake hands.

If you visit a family, a small bunch of flowers would be a good present. You should take the wrapping paper off them before handing them over. When eating with a German family, keep your hands on the table when not actually eating.

Finally, you may well find that a lot of German teenagers have a good deal of independence. Some of them even have their own part of the house. Often parents convert the cellar into a self-contained apartment for their children.

SUPERQUIZ

1. What is **der Schwarzwald** in English?

2. What is **Sachertorte**?

3. What does **Auskunft** mean?

4. How many **Groschen** are there in an Austrian **Schilling**?

5. What could you buy in a **Konditorei**?

6. What is a **Rabbit Card**?

7. What does **Einzelfahrschein** mean?

8. What do you need to book into a youth hostel?

9. What is the difference between a **Hallenbad** and a **Freibad**?

10. Where can you buy medicine?

11. What is a **Wiener Schnitzel**?

12. What does it mean in a café if you are asked **"mit oder ohne?"**

13. What is a **Schnellimbiß**?
